Circuits

Theodore Buchanan

Consultant

Michael Patterson
Principal Systems Engineer

Publishing Credits

Rachelle Cracchiolo, M.S.Ed., *Publisher*
Conni Medina, M.A.Ed., *Managing Editor*
Diana Kenney, M.A.Ed., NBCT, *Senior Editor*
Dona Herweck Rice, *Series Developer*
Robin Erickson, *Multimedia Designer*
Timothy Bradley, *Illustrator*

Image Credits: Cover, p.1 Henrik5000 /iStock;
p.27 Chetan Bansal / Alamy; p.23 Douglas W. Jones /
Wikimedia Commons; p.10 Getty Images / Lonely Planet
Images; pp.2, 5, 6, 7, 8, 11, 13, 14, 16, 17, 18, 19, 20, 23, 25,
32 iStock; pp.28, 29 J.J. Rudisill; p.24 KPA/United Archives/
WHA/Newscom; p.26 Nathan Barry; p.19 Newscom; p.25
Richard Luria / Science Source; pp.9, 12, 15, 16, 20, 21
Travis Hanson; all other images from Shutterstock.

Library of Congress Cataloging-in-Publication Data

Buchanan, Theodore, author.
 Circuits / Theodore Buchanan.
  pages cm
 Summary: "Have you ever wondered how the
human brain works? What about your television? It's
a complicated answer, but circuits are a simple way to
explain it. Circuits make it possible to turn on a light.
They make is possible for you to use your digital devices.
Increase your knowledge about circuits and find the
answers to your most electrifying questions"-- Provided
by publisher.
 Audience: Grades 4-6.
 Includes index.
 ISBN 978-1-4807-4682-4 (pbk.)
1. Electric circuits--Juvenile literature. 2. Electricity--
Juvenile literature. I. Title.
 TK148.B938 2016
 621.319'2--dc23
                                    missing last #

Teacher Created Materials

5301 Oceanus Drive
Huntington Beach, CA 92649-1030
http://www.tcmpub.com

ISBN 978-1-4807-4682-4

Table of Contents

Loop de Loops

Neon signs flashing. Computers blip-blip-beeping. Toasters popping. Music soaring. Our world is filled with electricity and its effects.

What shapes, moves, and controls all this electricity? **Circuits!** A circuit is a loop. It creates a path for electric **current** to flow.

Simple things such as flashlights are made up of just one circuit. Other more complex machines, such as computers, are made up of thousands of circuits. Circuits can be teeny-tiny or cover miles of ground. But no matter the size or complexity, circuits affect our world in powerful ways.

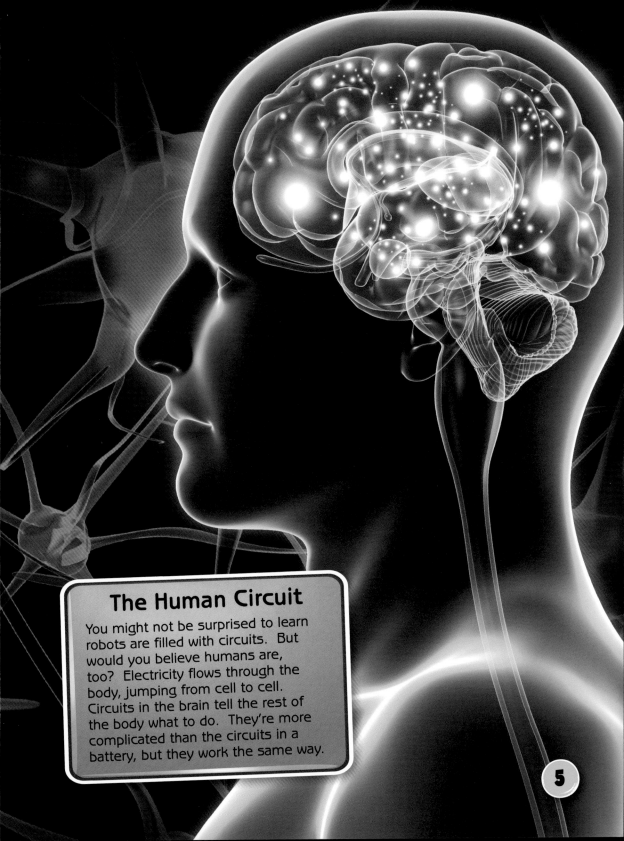

The Human Circuit

You might not be surprised to learn robots are filled with circuits. But would you believe humans are, too? Electricity flows through the body, jumping from cell to cell. Circuits in the brain tell the rest of the body what to do. They're more complicated than the circuits in a battery, but they work the same way.

Zipping and Zapping

Electricity is usually invisible, and that might make it seem mysterious. But scientists have been studying it for hundreds of years. Along the way, they've learned some amazing things.

All matter is made of tiny particles called *atoms*. Atoms make up everything from electric eels to lightbulbs. These atoms are very small. Billions of them can fit on the period at the end of a sentence.

Even smaller particles called *protons, neutrons,* and *electrons* make up atoms. The protons and neutrons cluster to form the nucleus, which is located at the center of the atom. Electrons are smaller and lighter. They move around the nucleus. Protons have a positive charge. Electrons have a negative charge. Neutrons have no charge.

Electrons are always moving. They jump easily from one atom to another. When the flow of electrons is constant, it creates an electric current.

It takes 6,000,000,000,000,000,000 electrons to light a 100-watt lightbulb for just one second.

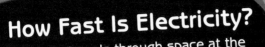

How Fast Is Electricity?

Electricity travels through space at the speed of light! That's 1,079,252,848 kilometers per hour (670,616,629 miles per hour)! It moves about 1/100th of this speed when it travels through electrical wires. That's still too fast for humans to see!

A Simple Circuit

So, where do all these electrons go when they're zipping around? Many travel through circuits. A circuit is formed when a power source is connected to something that receives the current.

Scientists often try to understand simple situations before they tackle more complex issues. So, let's take a look at a very simple circuit. All it includes is a wire, a lightbulb, and a battery. The electric current travels from the battery through the wire to the lightbulb.

The most important thing about this circuit is that it forms a complete loop. As soon as one part is removed or a wire is disconnected, the lightbulb stops working.

Electric Ink

You don't always need wires to create a circuit. Scientists have discovered other materials that can be used to form circuits. There's even a special kind of ink you can use to draw a circuit!

Special ink can make a circuit

Cut Out the Clutter

When studying circuits, it's useful to make simple diagrams that show exactly how the circuit works—and nothing else. A schematic diagram like the one below shows only the main parts. Standard symbols help engineers quickly draw diagrams.

A dot or a circle is placed in the diagram to show where the lightbulb connects.

Straight lines indicate wires.

This symbol indicates a battery.

9

Scientists don't just design circuits with current flowing through them. They measure the current, too. This helps them predict and control it.

Voltage is like pressure that pushes an electric current through a wire. The concept is similar to water pressure. Have you ever tried to wash your hair when the water pressure is too low? It's difficult to get the shampoo out of your hair. High levels of water pressure can be too intense, though. You don't want to get washed down the drain! Electrical pressure works the same way. Low voltage produces weak effects. But high levels of voltage can deliver a strong zap.

Amperes (amps) are a measure of the number of electrons flowing past a point per second. Just like more raindrops make for a more powerful storm, more electrons result in a stronger current.

Electric eels use electricity to defend themselves. They can produce an electric shock of up to 600 volts with just one amp.

Measuring Amps

Electricians use a multimeter to measure amps. Here's how they do it. **Note:** Never test electricity on your own!

1. First, electricians look at the multimeter to see how many amps it can measure. Some models can only handle up to 10 amps, while others can measure 200!

2. To test household power, they set the multimeter to AC (alternating current). To test a battery, they set it to DC (direct current).

3. Then, they set the range on the multimeter. The range is the sensitivity to amps.

4. Next, electricians turn off any circuit breakers. They connect the multimeter to the circuit.

5. Then, they turn the breaker back on. If a reading is not produced on the multimeter, they change the range.

6. Finally, when they're done, they turn the breaker off again before removing and rewiring the circuit.

Be Careful!

- Electricity can shock you. Always wear heavy rubber gloves.

- Do not work in a wet environment. Electricity is conducted through water.

- Read the owner's manual entirely to make sure that you are using electrical devices correctly.

All About Analog

Today, we're surrounded by touch screens, remote controls, and flashy video games. These high-tech devices are all powered by **digital** circuits. But no one could have developed a digital circuit without first conquering the parts and pieces of analog circuits. After all, all digital circuits are analog, but not all analog circuits are digital.

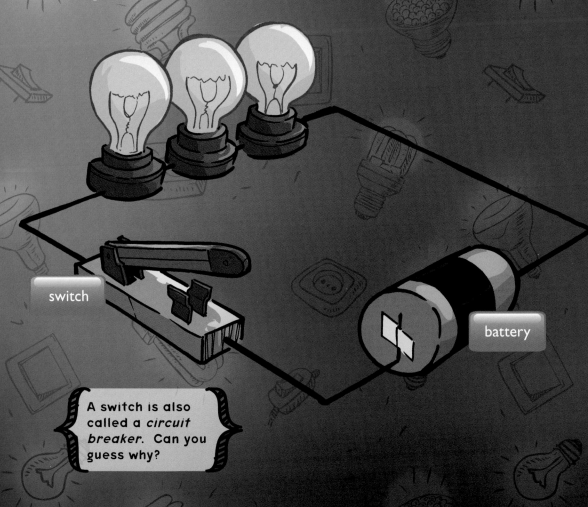

switch

battery

A switch is also called a *circuit breaker*. Can you guess why?

Series Circuits

A **series circuit** has only one electrical pathway. That's why they're easy to make! Everything you need in the circuit can be lined up on the same wire. But that means that if one component fails, they all do.

The diagram on the left shows a string of lights that are in a series circuit. All the lightbulbs are lined up in a long series. Unfortunately, they don't always work well. Like batteries, lightbulbs don't last forever. Over time, the filament, which is a small piece of metal that lights the bulb, will burn out. This breaks the circuit.

Switches

What good is a lightbulb if it can't be turned on and off? Switches open and close a circuit. Switches can be used to turn a lightbulb off. When the circuit is broken, the electricity can't flow. It's just like when a bulb burns out in a series circuit. It breaks the electrical flow. If one bulb burns out, all the bulbs go dark.

Parallel Circuits

Parallel circuits have more than one electrical pathway to move along. If there is more than one path, then it's a parallel circuit—hence the name. Most households are wired with parallel circuits. That way, if one bulb goes out, it doesn't take the whole circuit with it. You wouldn't want all the lights in your house to go out when you turn off the TV. Parallel circuits keep the lights on.

There are multiple paths electricity can take in a parallel circuit. As electric current travels the loop, it must enter through a single **resistor**. By the laws of physics, it has to travel through the path of least resistance. If the current for both paths is the same, then it will split evenly through each resistor. If one resistor is disconnected, then it will choose the other path. This is what allows the circuit to continue.

Beware of Overload!

Think about your home. If you plug a bunch of cords into the wall (a parallel circuit) the resistance is lowered. Remember, when the resistance decreases, the total current increases. So when you plug more cords in, the current must increase. If you plug too many in, it can be dangerous!

Parallel or Series?

Compare a parallel to a series circuit using a 9-volt battery, tape, aluminum foil, two lightbulbs—and the help of an adult!

1. Tape one 8-inch strip of foil to the positive end and another to the negative end of the 9-volt battery.

2. Wrap the foil that is attached to the positive end around one lightbulb. Wrap a 4-inch strip of foil around both lightbulbs.

3. Touch the second lightbulb to the foil connected to the negative end. This is a series circuit! Try removing one lightbulb from the circuit. What happens to the other?

4. Remove the lightbulbs from the circuit. Wrap two 4-inch strips of foil around the foil coming from the positive end.

5. Wrap the other ends of these strips around the lightbulbs. Touch the lightbulbs to the foil connected to the negative end. This is a parallel circuit. Try removing one lightbulb from the circuit. What happens to the other?

6. Which type of circuit is more useful? Which makes the light burn brighter?

Complex Circuits

We've looked at series circuits. We've looked at parallel circuits. But circuits aren't always that simple. Sometimes, they have both series and parallel parts. These are complex circuits. It's useful to study simple series circuits and parallel circuits because they help us understand how electricity works. But most electronics have complex circuits. Computers have complex circuits. So do phones!

Exploring Circuitry

Studying circuits can lead to everything from a simple hobby at home to a full-time career. Circuit designers usually work for technology companies, designing circuits for products. Using their knowledge of circuits, some even design lighting for shows in the theater or places such as Disneyland.

Bird on a Wire

If a bird lands on a power line and touches two lines at the same time, it can complete an electrical circuit, sending electricity through the bird and giving it an unexpected shock!

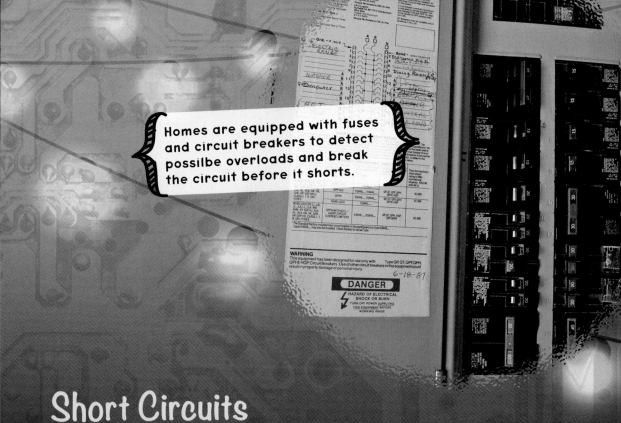

Homes are equipped with fuses and circuit breakers to detect possilbe overloads and break the circuit before it shorts.

Short Circuits

A short circuit occurs when a part of a circuit is not connected properly. The illustration to the right shows a poorly made circuit. Here, one of the basic parts of a circuit is missing. A circuit should include a power source, a connection, and the object receiving the power. But here, the power source and the object receiving the power are the same thing: a battery. Instead of sending the electricity through a lightbulb, the circuit directs it to take a shortcut. It travels from one end of the battery to the next. The battery gets a large jolt of electricity, it overheats, and a fire may start.

Controlling Circuits

Whether they're building a series, parallel, or complex circuit, scientists choose their materials carefully.

Some materials allow electricity to flow more easily than others. Silver, gold and copper all do this. Water does, too. These materials all conduct electricity well. **Conductors** are made of atoms with loose electrons that can move easily. Metals are some of the best conductors. That's why the wires in many circuits are made of copper.

But wires are usually wrapped in rubber. Why would that be? Rubber is an **insulator**, the opposite of a conductor. It doesn't conduct electricity well. The atoms in insulators have close-knit rings of electrons that are hard to move. They prevent electricity from flowing. Glass, wood, and plastic are all good examples of insulators.

Insulators are important. They keep us from getting shocked. They also tend not to carry heat. A metal slide on a playground may get hot in the sun. Plastic usually doesn't get as hot. A pan may get hot on the stove, but a plastic handle stays cooler. Plastic is the most common insulator. But it doesn't work for everything. For larger jobs with a higher amount of electricity, a material similar to pottery is often used.

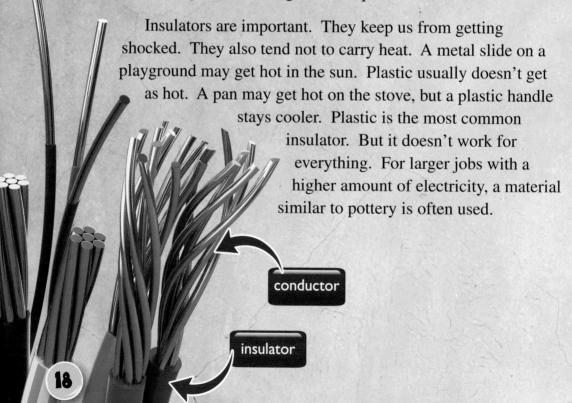

conductor

insulator

18

Capacitors

Capacitors are similar to batteries, but batteries produce energy and capacitors store and release energy. If there is too much electricity entering a capacitor, it will store the extra energy to use later.

Smart phones use capacitors in touch screens. Electrodes, or points where electricity flows, are built into the screen of a touchscreen phone.

When you touch the capacitor, the current is drawn to your finger.

The computer in the phone identifies the location of the touch and tells the phone what to do.

Resistors

The purpose of a resistor within a circuit is to make the current's flow smaller. But resistors do more than just dim lightbulbs. Resistors adjust current so it can be used in complex circuits.

resistor

Going Digital

Analog circuits are used in everything from toasters to **amplifiers**. They can be elegant and complex. But digital circuits allow designers to be even more flexible. The same rules that apply to analog circuits apply to digital circuits. And digital circuits can do all the same things that analog circuits can do. But they can also do more.

Analog Versus Digital

analog

The microphone turns the sound waves into an electrical signal.

Sound waves travel to a microphone.

digital

Sound waves are translated into a digital signal made up of ones and zeroes.

Most of the music we listen to is stored digitally. This format allows us to store a lot of information (or songs) on a small device. It's easier to move and send the information over large distances. However, some music lovers prefer the old analog format. This is because when music is converted into a digital format, some of the highest and lowest sounds are lost. This makes it fit on a small device, but it does not sound as rich.

The signal goes through an amplifier, which boosts the signal.

A speaker vibrates the air, which creates a sound wave.

The digital signal is stored in a computer.

The digital signal is then translated and sent to speakers, which vibrate the air.

Digital circuits can be made very small. Do you have an old remote control lying around the house? Take a look inside, and you'll find a green printed circuit board (PCB). PCBs are thin boards made of plastic. Copper wires connect all the components on the board. Copper is used because it's a good conductor. Once all the wires are **fused** onto the board, they form closed loops. These are tiny circuits.

Once a power supply runs through the wires, the board can control every component. This type of technology is used today in cell phones, digital cameras, and tablets.

Integrated Circuits

With the use of a new type of circuit called *integrated circuits*, we can conduct electricity better every year. The size of the circuit gets smaller, but the amount of electricity it can conduct gets larger. Today, integrated circuits that fit in your phone have more power than circuits in computers that used to fill a whole room!

integrated circuit

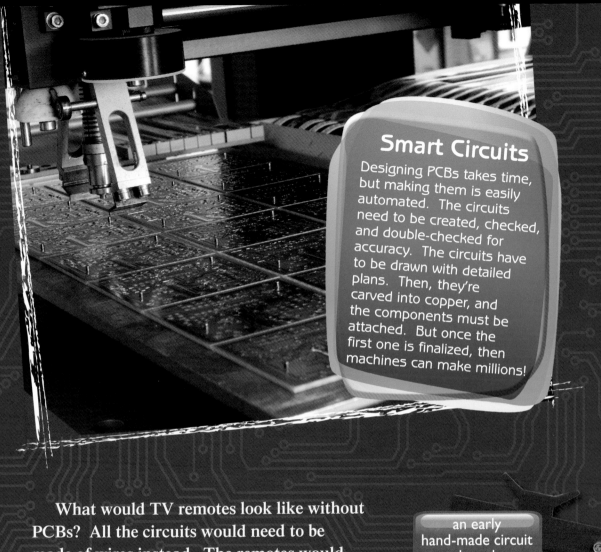

Smart Circuits

Designing PCBs takes time, but making them is easily automated. The circuits need to be created, checked, and double-checked for accuracy. The circuits have to be drawn with detailed plans. Then, they're carved into copper, and the components must be attached. But once the first one is finalized, then machines can make millions!

What would TV remotes look like without PCBs? All the circuits would need to be made of wires instead. The remotes would be enormous—and hard to use. Who wants to haul a 12-inch remote control on to the couch? Might as well get up and change the channel! PCBs allow engineers to make smaller and smaller gadgets. They have even created flex boards. You guessed it . . . they're flexible! This allows the board to fit into odd places and opens up opportunities for new technology.

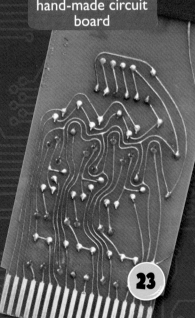

an early hand-made circuit board

23

Power On!

Electricity can be generated from wind, water, the sun, and even animal waste! Many electronics, however, rely on simple batteries.

Batteries are used as a mobile energy source. A chemical reaction inside the battery produces an abundance of electrons. When the circuit is closed, the electrons travel from the negative end of the battery to the positive end. Batteries die when the chemicals in the middle run out. No more electrons means no more electricity.

Bigger batteries may last longer. But with time, all batteries will run out. So a lot of electronics have plugs instead. They plug into sockets that get electricity from power plants. This creates circuits in a similar way. Electrons flow through one prong in the plug. Then, they travel through a wire and reach what needs to be powered. Once there, they flow back through another wire in the same cord and travel out the other prong.

What's the real energy that powers circuits? Brain power! Building a successful circuit requires careful planning. There's a certain logic to working with electronics. You know if the volts go up, the current increases. If you add more switches, you can break the circuit in more places. Electricians use what they know about electricity to craft complex and precise circuits. Now that's a bright idea!

Alessandro Volta invented the first battery in 1800. The first rechargeable battery was invented by Gaston Plante, pictured here, in 1859.

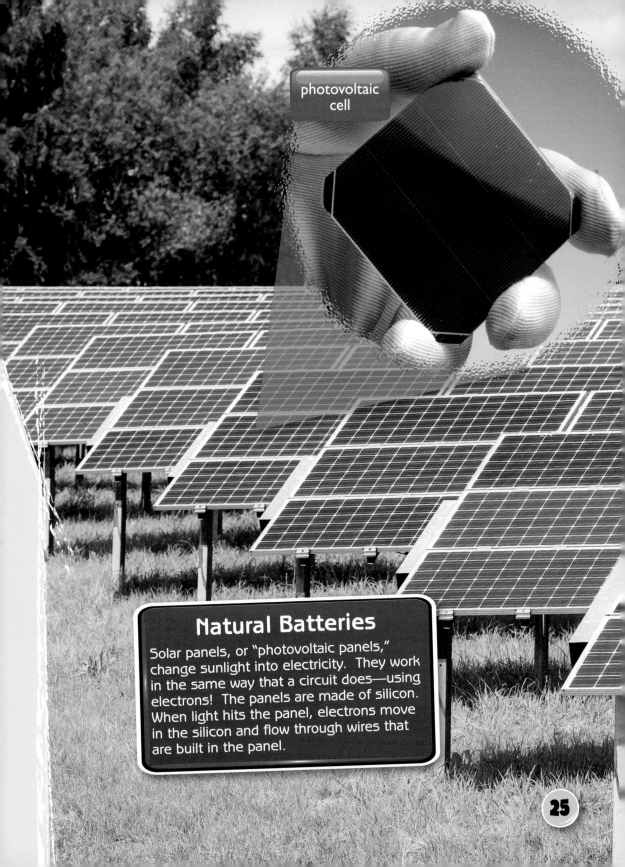

photovoltaic
cell

Natural Batteries

Solar panels, or "photovoltaic panels,"
change sunlight into electricity. They work
in the same way that a circuit does—using
electrons! The panels are made of silicon.
When light hits the panel, electrons move
in the silicon and flow through wires that
are built in the panel.

Coming Full Circuit

Circuits come in many different forms. They power everything from simple lightbulbs to high-tech jets. It may have taken thousands of years for people to understand electricity. But today, we know that with a little power and a few wires, we can turn nearly *anything* into a circuit. Bananas. Dough. Even pencils have been used to make circuits!

Engineers are finding new places to put circuits, too. In the future, it might not be unusual to find circuits in your clothes. With a little bit of tinkering, devices with circuits could be designed to protect us from the sun, help us exercise, and monitor our health.

It's easy to experiment with circuits. And today, new technology is allowing artists, scientists, and other creative thinkers to paint circuits on glass, fabric, and even skin. So why not power up and see what you can make? The world is your circuit!

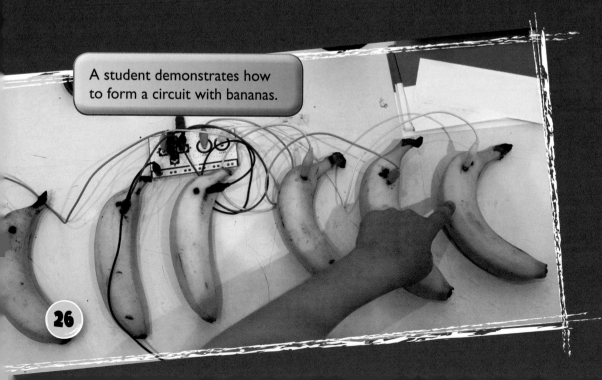

A student demonstrates how to form a circuit with bananas.

electroluminescent wire
used as shoelaces

Think Like a Scientist

How can you use a lemon to power a lightbulb? Experiment and find out!

What to Get

- 1 set of twinkle lights with a 2-inch lead of wire
- 2 inches of wire
- copper nail
- lemon
- zinc nail

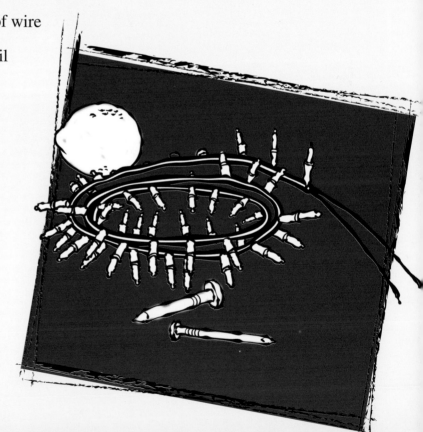

What to Do

1 Roll the lemon on a table to soften it and to loosen the juices.

2 Insert the zinc and copper nails into the lemon two inches apart. Don't let them go through the outside of the lemon.

3 Remove the insulation from the string of lights. You should be able to see the wire underneath.

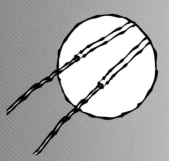

4 Wrap one wire around each nail.

5 Observe what happens. Where do you think the lemon gets its energy? How is this similar to a battery?

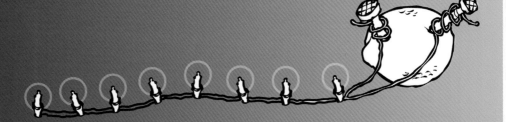

Glossary

amperes—units for measuring the rate at which electric current flows

amplifiers—devices that increase the strength of electric signals so that sounds played through an electronic system are louder

circuits—complete paths that electric currents travel along

conductors—materials or objects that allow electricity or heat to move through them

current—a flow of electricity

digital—using or characterized by computer technology

fused—joined or blended together

insulator—a material that allows little or no heat, electricity, or sound to go into or out of something

parallel circuits—electrical circuits that have more than one pathway for electricity to follow

resistor—a device that is used to control the flow of electricity in an electric circuit

series circuit—an electrical circuit that has only one path for electricity to follow

voltage—the force of an electrical current that is measured in volts

Index

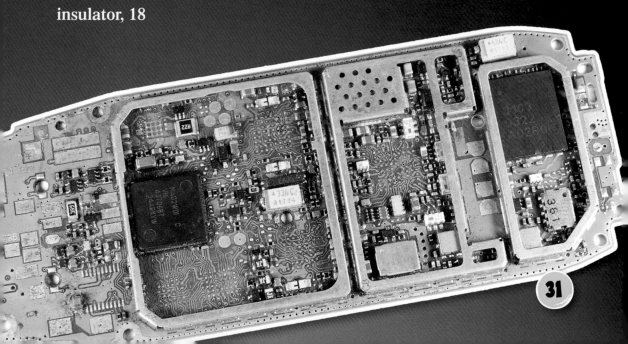

Your Turn!

Observing Circuits

Observe circuits at work! Find a string of decorative lights that operate on a series circuit. Find another string of lights that have a parallel circuit. Remove a lightbulb from each string. What happens to the other lights? What are the pros and cons of the series circuit? What are the pros and cons of the parallel circuit?